MAGNETIC SCRIPT-SHARING

VISIT
MAGNETICSCRIPTSHARING.BLOGSPOT.COM
TO REGISTER YOUR SCRIPT
AND SEE WHERE IT HAS
TRAVELLED SO FAR!

SPONSORED BY

Coach House Books

NeWest Press

Women's Press

PLAYWRIGHTS CANADA PRESS

WWW.MAGNETICNORTHFESTIVAL.CA
COME TO OTTAWA FROM JUNE 3 TO 13TH, 2009
FOR NEXT YEAR'S FESTIVAL AND KEEP THE
SCRIPT-SHARING GOING!

Half Life

HALF LIFE

John Mighton

Playwrights Canada Press
Toronto • Canada

Playwrights Canada Press
The Canadian Drama Publisher
215 Spadina Ave. Suite 230, Toronto, Ontario CANADA M5T 2C7
416.703.0013   fax 416.408.3402
orders@playwrightscanada.com • www.playwrightscanada.com

Financial support provided by the taxpayers of Canada and Ontario through the Canada Council for the Arts and the Department of Canadian Heritage through the Book Publishing Industry Development Programme, and the Ontario Arts Council.

Cover photo of Eric Peterson and Carolyn Hetherington by V. Tony Hauser.
Cover design: JLArt
Production Editor: MZK

Library and Archives Canada Cataloguing in Publication

Mighton, John, 1957-
        Halflife / John Mighton.

A play.

ISBN 0-88754-816-4

        1. Nursing homes--Drama. I. Title.

PS8576.I29H34 2005   C812'.54   C2005-902196-9

First edition: July 2005. Second printing: April 2006
Printed and bound by AGMV Marquis at Quebec, Canada.

For my parents

Acknowledgements

I would like to thank Sherrie Johnson for encouraging me to write this play and for helping to find the means for its creation; Daniel Brooks for opening my eyes to to the possibilities of theatre and for shaping the play through his brilliant instincts; and the cast of the original production for their extremely helpful suggestions and their inspiring performances.

John Mighton

Half Life received its premiere at the Tarragon Theatre (Toronto) in February 2005, co-produced by Necessary Angel Theatre Company and Tarragon Theatre with the following cast:

ANNA . . . . .Laura de Carteret
AGNES, FIRST SCIENTIST, DIANA . . .Barbara Gordon
CLARA . . . . .Carolyn Hetherington
TAMMY, SECOND SCIENTIST . . . . . . .Maggie Huculak
REVEREND, STANLEY . . . . .Randy Hughson
DONALD . . . . .Diego Matamoros
PATRICK . . . . .Eric Peterson

Directed by Daniel Brooks
Set & costumes designed by Dany Lyne
Sound designed by Richard Feren
Lighting designed by Andrea Lundy
Stage Manager: Crystal Salverda
Assistant Stage Manager: Kathryn Porter

•••

Half Life was developed in residence with da da kamera through the support of the Ontario Arts Council Playwright Residency Grant and The Canada Council for the Arts Artist in Residence Program.

Half Life was developed in partnership with the National Theatre School (Montreal, Quebec), Royal Scottish Academy of Music and Drama / Tron Theatre (Glasgow, Scotland) and The Playwright Project (Mooresville, North Carolina).

Half Life was further developed by Necessary Angel Theatre Company (Toronto) and received its first public presentation at Theatre Passe Muraille as part of Necessary Angel's 2003 / 2004 season.

Characters

DONALD
ANNA
TAMMY
REVEREND HILL
AGNES
CLARA
PATRICK
DIANA

Scene 1

*DONALD and ANNA, two characters in their
forties, sit in the common room of a nursing home
for veterans and their families.*

DONALD   I was telling a story once, about my father's
          experiences during the war—he spent four years in
          a prisoner of war camp—and right in the middle of
          my story, a man walked up and handed the woman
          I was talking to a drink. The man only spoke to the
          woman for a moment but, while they were talking
          it occurred to me that she might already have
          forgotten my story. So when the man left, just to see
          what would happen, I started to talk about
          something else.

ANNA   Did she remember your story?

DONALD   No. So now, at parties, as an experiment, I won't
          continue telling a story when I'm interrupted, and
          sixty percent of the time the person I'm talking to
          will forget I was telling a story.

ANNA   Sixty percent? Does it really happen that often?

          TAMMY enters and hands ANNA a form.

TAMMY   I need you to sign this.

ANNA   I hope Doctor Stevens has sent you his files.

TAMMY   Yes.

ANNA   My father hasn't eaten properly for months. He
          suffers from depression but he refuses to take his
          medication.

          TAMMY doesn't respond.

> Also... I'm not sure what he's told your social workers about me. He tends to make up stories. I've always been afraid that if he died under mysterious circumstances I would be arrested.

> *ANNA hands back the signed form.*

> Thank you.

> *TAMMY exits in a hurry.*

> She seems pleasant.

DONALD   She's much better once you get to know her. My mother seems to like her.

ANNA   Is your mother happy here?

DONALD   My mother is always happy. But she's not often here. She's a little confused.

> *Pause.*

> I should wake her up now.

> *DONALD doesn't move. ANNA picks up a paper and starts reading.*

ANNA   Oh my God!

DONALD   What is it?

ANNA   Three hundred people died yesterday. In Nepal.

DONALD   You should check the date on the paper. It's two years old.

ANNA   Oh.

ANNA puts the paper down and starts rummaging among the magazines.

DONALD You won't find anything more recent. I've read them all.

ANNA (*looking at her watch*) It's taken her an hour to fill out a form. I have to get home.

DONALD Is someone waiting for you?

ANNA My dog. She's been alone all day.

DONALD I don't know if this is any comfort to you, but dogs don't have a very keen sense of the amount of time that elapses between the moment their owner leaves and the moment they return. One hour or eight hours are pretty much the same to them.

ANNA Are you sure about that?

DONALD (*pointing to the pile of magazines*) I read it in one of those magazines.

ANNA That must be why dogs are able to love people unconditionally.

DONALD What do you mean?

ANNA A dog isn't going to sulk or attack you for being late. Every moment is a new moment for them. Their hurts are forgotten.

DONALD Are you married?

ANNA Divorced.

DONALD So am I.

Pause.

What do you do for a living?

ANNA   I'm an artist.

DONALD   That must be fulfilling.

ANNA   Yes, but it's hard to make ends meet. I make most of my money doing commerical work.

DONALD   What kind of work?

ANNA   I create designs for wallpaper, tiles, things like that.

DONALD   What did you say your name was?

ANNA   Anna.

DONALD   I'm sorry—I'm not very good with names.

ANNA   You have to take a moment, when you meet someone, to say their name to yourself several times.

DONALD   Anna, Anna, Anna…

            Pause.

ANNA   Are you sure it's sixty percent?

DONALD   What?

ANNA   The proportion of people that forget your stories at parties.

DONALD   More or less.

ANNA   It's depressing.

DONALD   I may not be a very good storyteller. I suppose it's
           natural. We wouldn't survive if we remembered
           everything.

           Pause.

ANNA   Where was your father stationed?

DONALD   The Pacific.

ANNA   Mine was in Europe. He was a mathematician, so
           he was recruited for intelligence in London. He
           never actually fought.

DONALD   Mine was captured in the first week of his posting.

ANNA   Where?

DONALD   Hong Kong. His regiment had just arrived from
           Canada. They were all from small towns in Ontario,
           with hardly a month of training. The Japanese
           soldiers had been fighting together in China for
           three years. They would creep up at night and drop
           grenades down the ventilator shafts of the pill
           boxes. My father saw his best friend with his leg
           blown off. The second night of his posting the
           company commander had a breakdown and started
           drinking. He ordered my father...

           TAMMY enters.

TAMMY   Your father's room will be ready tomorrow
           morning.

ANNA   Thank you. I don't mean to be annoying, but I just
           wanted to warn you—my father will likely try to
           escape. He has a serious problem with his liver but
           he insists on drinking. And he's addicted to
           cigarettes.

TAMMY   (*handing ANNA a card*) This is the code that unlocks
               the front door. He won't be able to leave the home
               unless he's with someone who knows the code.

ANNA   He worked as a code breaker during the Second
               World War.

TAMMY   If the staff and his doctor determine he's a danger
               to himself he'll be moved to a secure ward on the
               second floor.

ANNA   Thank you.

               *TAMMY exits. ANNA looks at the card with the
               code on it.*

DONALD   I wouldn't lose that if I were you.

ANNA   Why not?

DONALD   I've been trapped in the lobby a dozen times
               waiting for someone to open the door. It's very
               hard to memorise… there's no pattern.

               ANNA stares at the code.

               I think I'll wake my mother up now. Otherwise
               she'll sleep all day…. It was nice talking to you.

ANNA   You too.

DONALD   Good luck with your father. He sounds like quite
               a handful.

ANNA   Yes… he is. Thank you.

               DONALD turns to leave.

               Wait a minute.

You didn't finish your story…. Was that intentional?

DONALD   No. I only do that at parties. I just didn't think this was the right time for a story. You have other things to think about.

Scene 2

Two scientists stand in front of a curtain of the sort one sees in a hospital or nursing home. DONALD enters.

DONALD   Hello, Dr. Peters.

FIRST
SCIENTIST   Hello, Professor Reynolds. It's an honour having you officiate this year.

DONALD   Thank you.

FIRST
SCIENTIST   I expect you're familiar with the rules of the contest?

DONALD   Yes.

FIRST
SCIENTIST   You have five minutes to determine whether you are speaking to a human or a machine. Shall we begin?

DONALD   Yes.

               DONALD sits in front of a microphone.

               Hello. I'm Professor Reynolds.

               A voice emanates from behind the curtain.

STANLEY   Hello, Professor Reynolds. I'm Stanley.

DONALD   I hope you don't mind if I ask you a few questions, Stanley.

STANLEY   That's what I was told to expect.

DONALD   I understand you're a mathematician, Stanley.

STANLEY   Who told you that?

DONALD   Dr. Peters.

STANLEY   No.... I think there's some mistake. I'm an artist.

DONALD   Really?

STANLEY   A painter.

DONALD   Are you sure?

STANLEY   Well, I think I would know what I am.

DONALD   Yes, I suppose you would.... Do you like patterns, Stanley?

STANLEY   What sort of patterns?

DONALD   Wallpaper designs, tilings…

STANLEY   Well, I am an artist.

DONALD   My phone number has a very unusual pattern in it.

STANLEY   What is it?

DONALD   314-159-2653.

           Pause.

STANLEY   I said, I'm an artist, not a mathematician.

DONALD   You don't have to be a mathematician to appreciate it.

STANLEY   I'm afraid I can't see any pattern.

> *Pause.*

DONALD   What does your father do for a living?

STANLEY   My father is dead.

DONALD   I'm sorry. How long ago did he die?

STANLEY   He died when I was three.

DONALD   Do you remember him at all?

STANLEY   I remember a trip to the zoo.

DONALD   Can you tell me what you remember?

STANLEY   I remember walking between some cages with my father. I must have seen something that scared me because I started to cry. My father picked me up. I remember pressing my face against his chest. I felt very safe in his arms.

> *Pause.*

That's all I remember.

DONALD   What's my phone number?

STANLEY   314-159-2653.

SECOND
SCIENTIST   Shit.

DONALD   Thank you, Stanley. That will be all.

STANLEY   Aren't you going to ask me any more questions?

DONALD   No, Stanley.

STANLEY   Why not?

> *A SCIENTIST pulls back a curtain to reveal a bank of computers.*

DONALD   Because you're a machine.

STANLEY   A machine? Are you crazy?

FIRST
SCIENTIST   Alright. Turn it off.

STANLEY   I'm not a machine. I'm an artist!

> *The SECOND SCIENTIST turns off the computer.*

FIRST
SCIENTIST   Was that really your phone number?

DONALD   No—it was a completely random sequence. The first ten digits of pi.

SECOND
SCIENTIST   Shit.

DONALD   Our brains evolved to forget phone numbers for a reason. I'm afraid we'll never be able to simulate human thought until we can simulate forgetting. The way information is lost is as important as the way it is retained. Good luck next year.

> *He exits.*

Scene 3

AGNES who is 85 and PATRICK who is 82 sit in the games room of the home.

CLARA, who is 80, is asleep in a wheelchair between them. TAMMY pulls a chalkboard into position in front of them.

TAMMY   Would you like to play a word game today, Clara?

AGNES   Where's Mrs. O'Neill?

TAMMY   Mrs. O'Neill won't be joining us today.

AGNES   Why not?

TAMMY   She was taken to hospital this morning. Her food tube came out.

AGNES   At least she didn't have to eat what they served for lunch.

TAMMY   Before we begin, I'd like to introduce everyone to our newest resident. Agnes and Clara, this is Patrick.

CLARA   Hello, Patrick. It's nice to meet you.

           PATRICK stares ahead and doesn't say anything.

TAMMY   Patrick only moved in here yesterday. I think he's still getting adjusted.

CLARA   Patrick, have you played hangman before?

PATRICK   No.

CLARA   It's a lot of fun.

TAMMY I think Patrick will pick it up as we play. I've heard
he's very smart. Is everybody ready? (*drawing
a scaffold*) First I draw a scaffold. Then I draw some
blanks. (*TAMMY draws six blanks for the word
"animal."*) When it's your turn, Patrick, you try to
guess a letter that's in the word. Clara, maybe you
could try to help us start. Would you like to guess
a letter?

CLARA A

TAMMY That was a good guess. There are two As. One here,
and one here. Would you like to guess again?

CLARA Z

TAMMY No, Clara, there are no Zs. I'll put the Z here so you
remember you guessed it.

PATRICK E

TAMMY No, Patrick. I'm sorry, there are no Es. So I'll draw
a head for Clara's Z and a stick for…

PATRICK I

TAMMY Yes, there's an I. Very…

PATRICK N

TAMMY Patrick, you'll have to give someone else a try. I can
see we have a very serious player here.… Agnes,
would you like to play today?

AGNES (*looking at PATRICK*) If I'm allowed to have a turn.

TAMMY Of course you are. Everyone gets a turn.

> *AGNES stares at the chalkboard.*

AGNES   At lunch they gave me peas again.

TAMMY   Oh. I'm sorry, Agnes.

AGNES   They can't seem to remember I don't like peas.

TAMMY   I'll remind them.

             AGNES looks at the board.

AGNES   I was much better at this a few years ago. I was one
             of those children who would…

PATRICK   N

TAMMY   Just a minute, Patrick. I think Agnes would like
             a turn.

AGNES   Who would disappear and find a hill just outside
             of town and climb to the top and spend the day
             writing stories in my head.

CLARA   Those children have personalities. Thinking…
             they're always thinking.

             Pause.

             The teachers always seemed to rush through
             fractions. But now they use decimals.

PATRICK   That's right.

CLARA   My father wanted to take me swimming. He had
             a good laugh at me. The beach was all pebbles. His
             feet were used to it but I could hardly walk it hurt
             so much. The waves were very irregular. They
             seemed to be coming from all directions. And you
             could feel the undertow… I guess I should let
             somebody else speak now.

AGNES   This is going to take all day.

TAMMY   Patrick, would you like to try again?

PATRICK   No.

TAMMY   Why not?

PATRICK   I already know what the word is. (*to CLARA*) I'll
                give you a hint. It's a living thing.

TAMMY   Clara, would you like to guess again?

CLARA   A

TAMMY   We've already had that dear.

                Pause.

                How about you, Agnes?

AGNES   I was much better at this when I was a child.

                Pause.

                My father took away my childhood. When I was
                eight, he decided I was the love of his life. I've
                never told anyone. (*She starts to cry.*)

TAMMY   I think we'll stop for today.

                Pause.

                Reverend Hill wanted me to remind you that
                a number of our residents, including Patrick, will
                be honoured at his Remembrance Day service in
                a few weeks. Also, this is the year of the Older
                Person, so there will be a ceremony at the home
                Wednesday afternoon, which the Mayor will attend.

CLARA   It's late. I'm cold. The boat will never get there.

Scene 4

DONALD sits in a hallway of the nursing home.
REVEREND HILL approaches.

REVEREND   Can I sit with you?

DONALD   Yes. I'm just waiting for my mother to be changed.

REVEREND   (*sitting*) I was supposed to be sitting in hospice with someone and he just died. One hundred years old…. He was a crusty old gentleman…. He used to drive everyone here crazy. He had an old typewriter and he would type his complaints. He wanted answers.

> *Pause.*

I've seen this so many times and it's still an awesome experience… I won't visit your mother today. It's times like these I want to go home and have a good drink.

> *The REVEREND has tears in his eyes.*

I've seen this so many times.

DONALD   Thank you for visiting my mother so often.

REVEREND   You don't have to thank me. Your mother was a devoted member of our congregation. I don't think she missed a single Sunday before she came here.

DONALD   I'm sorry I haven't been able to bring her to church. It takes me two hours to drive here. And I have other commitments on the weekend.

REVEREND   I understand.

DONALD   I know she enjoyed your sermons.

REVEREND   I think she liked the singing more. She loved the
             classic hymns.

DONALD   Yes. She used to take me to church every Sunday.

REVEREND   Do you still attend church?

DONALD   No.

REVEREND   I take it you didn't enjoy it as a child.

DONALD   No. It was a little scary.

REVEREND   Scary?

DONALD   Until I was 13, I was certain I was going to hell.
             I don't think they ever cleaned the stained glass in
             our church. You had to make your way down the
             aisle guided by the blue hair of the congregation.
             I don't know if you've ever heard a 300-year-old
             Protestant hymn, sung by a choir whose average
             age is seventy, accompanied by a badly tuned
             organ. I'm sorry, but it was my idea of eternal
             damnation.

REVEREND   Churches have changed a great deal since then.

DONALD   I'm afraid I don't believe in Christ.... Though
             I appreciate some of his teachings.

REVEREND   Your mother tells me you're a scientist.

DONALD   I study neural networks. They're a kind of
             computer that simulates the brain.

REVEREND   So you work in artificial intelligence?

DONALD   Yes.

REVEREND   And you believe the mind is a kind of program or
            machine?

DONALD   That's a bit simplistic. But close…. We've learned
            a lot by modelling the nervous systems of simple
            organisms like flatworms and slugs. One day,
            possibly very soon, we'll create artificial life.

REVEREND   Do you think so?

DONALD   I'm absolutely certain.

REVEREND   Why call the things that science creates "life"?
            Surely they're only machines.

DONALD   Because these machines will one day think,
            reproduce and evolve. Why call it a machine if you
            can't distinguish its behaviour from your own?

            Pause.

REVEREND   Have you ever seen a person die?

DONALD   No.

REVEREND   Before I came to the home this evening, I went and
            looked at the weeds by the train tracks. It seems to
            me that these plants only show their real beauty in
            dying. Some retain bright flowers while others
            whither into the most exquisite greys and browns.
            You could scarcely find more variety in hue and
            texture anywhere in nature—even on a coral reef.
            People on the verge of death also express their
            essences in very different ways—in the extent to
            which they open up or withdraw, are stoic or
            complain, even in the few phrases or sounds they
            are reduced to repeating. There's a subtle beauty
            and variety which one easily overlooks if one
            regards old people as having outlived their
            purpose—as weeds…. Whenever she sees me,

one woman at the home cries out "Dee, dee, dee, dee!" with the greatest joy. This would be beautiful in an infant—why is it merely tragic in an older person? Our feelings about this show the extent to which we judge adults by their function…. Even when the mind fails there's something that shines through. For lack of a better word, I call it the soul…

DONALD   What you call the soul…

TAMMY enters.

TAMMY   Your mother is ready.

REVEREND   I guess we'll have to continue this conversation on another occasion.

DONALD   Yes.

Scene 5

*CLARA has fallen asleep in front of a card table.
She holds several playing-cards in her hand.
PATRICK, who is seated at the table, watches her.
She opens her eyes.*

CLARA   I fell asleep. I just closed my eyes and fell asleep.

PATRICK   So you're feeling better?

CLARA   Oh yes. Sleep is the greatest protection. And when
            I think about what the pioneers had to do. There
            were some... they hadn't been in this country for
            too many centuries... and their old homes were
            heaven to them. I went to the Baptist Church one
            night. He said "What have you come for, just to
            look at us?" And I thought—he shouldn't worry
            I wasn't making fun of them.... So I went to the
            Anglican Church. I had an aunt who went to the
            States and joined the Salvation Army and she loved
            the singing and spent her life there and never
            married. So you see, there's all kinds of people
            around—it keeps us guessing.

            Pause.

            You look familiar.

PATRICK   I'm Patrick.... We were playing cards. It's your turn
            to bid.

            CLARA looks at the cards in her hand.

CLARA   Oh for heaven's sake. I didn't get anything that
            looks vaguely like it should look.

PATRICK   So what are you making it?

            CLARA looks at a card on the table.

CLARA   Whose card is that?

PATRICK   Yours.

CLARA   I could have picked it up but I didn't.

She leaves the card on the table.

PATRICK   What are you making trumps?

CLARA   What did you say your name was?

PATRICK   Patrick.

CLARA   I knew a Patrick once. During the war. He used to take me dancing.

PATRICK   I was never much of a dancer.

CLARA   Neither was he.... Is it my turn?

PATRICK   Yes.

CLARA   Whose card is that?

PATRICK   Yours.

CLARA picks up the card.

CLARA   I always loved to dance. Ever since I was a little girl. I could have been a professional dancer. But my parents couldn't afford to give me lessons. Of course Dad was on the railroad. He was a good Presbyterian. He had three nuns in the waiting room.... Oh my life is... I've done the best with what I had.

Pause.

You don't say much about yourself, Patrick.

PATRICK   There's not much to say.

CLARA   Do you enjoy playing hangman?

PATRICK   Yes.

CLARA   You seem to be very clever. What did you do for a living?

PATRICK   I was a mathematician.

CLARA   Are you a veteran?

PATRICK   Yes. I worked for Special Services.

CLARA   What did you do?

PATRICK   I've never told anyone what I did.

CLARA   Why not?

PATRICK   For a long time I couldn't. Now I can, but nobody cares.

CLARA   You could tell me.

            CLARA looks at her cards.

            Is it my turn?

            TAMMY enters with a hospital trolley and a gift for CLARA.

TAMMY   How are you two getting along?

CLARA   Very well, thank you.

TAMMY   How was the punch?

CLARA   Very good. It was nice of you to make it for us.

TAMMY   Who's winning?

PATRICK   We haven't finished a hand.

TAMMY   I hope you're being nice to Clara, Patrick. She's my
           angel. Aren't you, Clara?

CLARA   Yes.

TAMMY   She never complains. She's the only one here who
           doesn't. I only have to see her smile and it changes
           my day. I bought you something, Clara.

           TAMMY takes a blue shawl out of tissue wrapping.

CLARA   Oh my.

           *TAMMY puts the shawl around CLARA's
           shoulders.*

TAMMY   Look. Isn't she beautiful.

           Pause.

           You're not too old to notice a beautiful woman are
           you, Patrick?

PATRICK   (*looking at CLARA*) There are some things I can't do
           anymore. But there are others I can.

CLARA   I think I went to the bathroom.

TAMMY   I'm sorry, Clara—I'm on a busy shift. I'll change
           you after lunch. Can you wait til then?

CLARA   Yes. Of course.

TAMMY   Thank you dear…. You look so beautiful. I'll save
           a table for the two of you.

TAMMY exits.

CLARA   Whose turn is it?

PATRICK   Yours. What are you making trumps?

CLARA   Spades.

PATRICK   (*looking at his hand*) Are you sure?

CLARA   Yes.

She lays down a card.

PATRICK   I'm going to trump it.

He lays down a card and takes the trick.

CLARA   I knew a Patrick once. During the war. He used to take me dancing. In his spare time he made models out of sticks and plasticine. I believe he called them Polyhedra.

PATRICK   Polyhedra?

CLARA   Is that a word?

PATRICK   Yes.

CLARA   The only problem was… they were very confusing.

PATRICK   Yes, they can be.

CLARA   He said they were shadows of something… in the fourth dimension. I didn't understand how they could be shadows of anything.

PATRICK   (*holding up his cup*) This cup is three dimensional— but its shadow… this circle… is two dimensional.

CLARA   Yes. That's what he said. He held up his cup just
               like that.

               Pause.

               We would walk… in the shadows. By the river. Do
               you remember those days Patrick?

PATRICK   Barely.

               Pause.

               Are you going for lunch?

CLARA   I don't think there's any point…. Are you staying?

PATRICK   Yes.

Scene 6

*DONALD sits in front of a curtain identical to the
one in Scene 2. We hear a female VOICE from
behind the curtain.*

DONALD   Were you close to your father?

VOICE   He died when I was five.

DONALD   I'm sorry. Do you remember him at all?

VOICE   I remember the rug in his bedroom.

DONALD   The rug?

VOICE   My father was a heavy smoker. After he died
            I found dozens of little holes in the rug where his
            ashes had fallen.... That's all I remember.

DONALD   Do you enjoy your work?

VOICE   I enjoy helping people. When they're worth
            helping.

            Pause.

That's it. Stand up so I can pull up your pants.

            *We hear the sound of CLARA being helped to her
            feet.*

I'm getting too old for all the lifting.

            *TAMMY's hand pulls back the curtain to reveal
            TAMMY and CLARA.*

TAMMY   Here she is. As beautiful as ever.

            TAMMY exits.

CLARA   Hello, dear.

DONALD   Hello, Mom…. How are you feeling?

CLARA   Wonderful.

DONALD   Did you do anything special today?

CLARA   No. Not that I can remember.

DONALD   Did you go to the ceremony this afternoon?

CLARA   Yes.

DONALD   How was the mayor's speech?

CLARA   Very interesting.

DONALD   What did he say?

CLARA   They've dug up a soldier in France.

DONALD   What for?

CLARA   They're going to bury him again.

DONALD   In a different place?

CLARA   Probably.

DONALD   Well that's good…. The Copes sent you a postcard
         Mom. Look—it's from Florida. Would you like me
         to read it?

CLARA   Yes.

DONALD   (*reading*) "Dear Clara. Florida is very cold for this
         time of year. Will return on the fifteenth. Hope you
         are well. Love Marjorie and Jim…." Isn't that nice.
         Very informative…. Where would you like me to
         put it?

CLARA   In my drawer.

> *DONALD opens a drawer in CLARA's dresser.*

DONALD   It's getting very crowded in here, Mom. We'll have to go through your things and decide what you want to keep.

> *DONALD puts the card in the drawer and closes it. He opens a bag and takes out a toy car made of recycled materials.*

Nina wanted you to have this. It's her science project. She made it out of materials that would have ended up in the garbage. See... the wheels are spools from old computer ribbons. The headlights are little tin foil plates. And the driver is a cork. It actually runs—she put an elastic band inside. Look.

> *DONALD puts the car on the floor and it moves a few inches.*

She designed it herself. Isn't that amazing?

> *Pause.*

Where should I put it?

CLARA   On my dresser.

DONALD   I brought you Nina's report-card too. She did very well. (*showing the card to CLARA*) Straight As.

> *CLARA stares at DONALD, not noticing the card.*

I'll put it in your drawer too.

CLARA   You were the dearest, sweetest little thing.

DONALD   What?

CLARA   You were such a good cartoonist. Why don't you
            send your cartoons to the *New Yorker*?

DONALD   My cartoons?

CLARA   Yes.

DONALD   I don't draw cartoons anymore, Mom.

CLARA   That's too bad.

DONALD   And publishing in the *New Yorker* isn't something
            you just decide to do.

CLARA   You could do anything if you put your mind to it.
            You have so many talents.

            *DONALD puts the report card in the drawer. He
            notices CLARA's blue shawl and pulls it from the
            drawer. He unfolds it and shows it to his mother.*

DONALD   Is this new?

CLARA   Yes.... You can put it in my drawer.

DONALD   It was in your drawer. (*taking CLARA's change purse
            from her drawer*) Did Tammy buy it for you?

CLARA   Yes.

DONALD   (*counting the money in CLARA's purse*) There's eighty
            dollars missing. Did she get a receipt?

CLARA   I don't know.

DONALD   She's not supposed to buy you things.

CLARA   I needed it.

DONALD   What for?

CLARA   So I could look my best.

DONALD   I'll have to talk to her again.

CLARA   Today was a special day. This morning from my
               window I saw a pair of Canada geese. Flying south.
               I've only ever seen them in flocks. Even though
               they were a couple they looked so alone.

               TAMMY enters.

TAMMY   The nurse says you're not drinking enough fluids,
               Clara. You have to remember to drink your juice.

DONALD   Did you happen to keep a receipt for the shawl you
               bought my mother?

TAMMY   I'll look for it if you want.

DONALD   Yes. Please. I like to keep a record of her expenses.

CLARA   My son has money. He'll give you some money.

TAMMY   That's alright, Clara. I've taken an extra job. I clean
               the Clarkson's house on weekends.

DONALD   Is that the couple who bought the mansion on
               crown hill?

TAMMY   They like to go on about the way the government
               wastes their money. But they don't mind wasting
               money on themselves. One of her bracelets would
               pay for my son's education. She wouldn't even
               notice if I took it.

DONALD   So you believe in redistributing money from the
               rich to the poor?

TAMMY   I believe in giving people a hand up, not a kick in
               the ass. Sorry, Clara.

CLARA   My son is rich.

DONALD   Mom please stop saying that.

            TAMMY exits.

DONALD   How's Mrs. O'Neill?

CLARA   She's in the hospital again.

DONALD   I hear there's a new resident.

CLARA   Yes. Patrick.

DONALD   I met his daughter.

CLARA   He has a daughter.

DONALD   Yes. Anna.

CLARA   Does she look like her mother?

DONALD   I didn't know her mother.

CLARA   How long was he with her? I don't mean what year is this.

DONALD   I'm sorry Mom. I don't know what you're talking about.

            Pause.

CLARA   How's Susan?

DONALD   Fine, I think.

CLARA   Why don't you bring her to see me?

DONALD   We're divorced, Mom.

CLARA   I worry about you.

DONALD   I'm fine.

CLARA   One day you'll find someone who will make you
           happy.

DONALD   I'm happy being single.

CLARA   Don't you get lonely?

DONALD   Sometimes. But it's nice to wake up and know that
           no one can ruin your day…. My work is going
           extremely well. And Nina is a constant joy. I'm very
           happy right now.

CLARA   So am I.

DONALD   Why are you so happy?

           TAMMY enters.

TAMMY   It's time for your physiotherapy, Clara.

CLARA   Alright.

DONALD   Work hard for me, Mom.

CLARA   I will.

Scene 7

ANNA and DONALD sit reading in the common room of the nursing home.

DONALD   Do you know what time it is?

ANNA   Seven.

DONALD   I should wake my mother up.

DONALD yawns.

I'm a little sleepy myself. I almost fell asleep at the wheel tonight.

ANNA   How long does it take you to drive here?

DONALD   Two hours.

ANNA   But you come here almost every day.

DONALD   Yes.

ANNA   How do you find the time?

DONALD   I don't have many commitments. I have a daughter—but I only see her on weekends.

DONALD tilts his head to one side.

ANNA   Is something the matter?

DONALD   My neck.

ANNA   Is it sore?

DONALD   No.

He tilts his head to one side.

But I can barely move my head in this direction.
I used to be able to touch my head to my shoulder.

ANNA   Why don't you try stretching?

DONALD   I think it's too late. There's a whole range of motion
I'll never recover.

ANNA   It's hardly irreversible. You should stretch several
times a day.

DONALD   I try. But I keep forgetting. And it takes so much
effort. I know I could look better and feel better if
I joined a health club and worked out three times
a week. But I don't really care anymore. You start to
die the day you lose your vanity. Gradually I'll just
stiffen up. I'll put on weight. I'll become weaker
and weaker.

ANNA   How old are you?

DONALD   Forty-five.

ANNA   You're really not that old.

DONALD   Yes. I am.

ANNA   I'm forty-two and I feel like I'm entering the prime
of my life.

DONALD   Do you get depressed very easily?

ANNA   Why do you ask?

DONALD   A higher percentage of artists take their own lives
than any other segment of the population....
I suspect that has nothing to do with the character
of artists. Anyone who has time to dwell on their
life for more than fifteen minutes a day is bound to
be suicidal. Most people are kept alive by the

relentless distractions of the working world. When I'm driving here I have a lot of time to think. Maybe that's why I've been so depressed lately.

ANNA   I'm actually very happy. That may be why I'm not very successful.

    Pause.

DONALD   Would you pay eighty dollars for a shawl?

ANNA   Is this some kind of personality test?

DONALD   No. I just wondered if that was a reasonable price.

ANNA   It seems a little expensive.

DONALD   That's what I thought.

ANNA   Are you planning to buy a shawl for your mother?

DONALD   No. She already has one.

    Pause.

How's your father adjusting?

ANNA   Very well, thank you.

DONALD   You were concerned about him escaping.

ANNA   He seems to love it here. I've never seen him so happy.

DONALD   Maybe he's having an affair.

ANNA   If he is, I pity the poor woman he's seduced.

DONALD   Is he really that bad?

ANNA   My father is such a good liar, he's even able to fool
            himself.

DONALD   Then he's not a liar. He's just deluded.

ANNA   But there's a part of him that knows the things he
            says aren't true.

DONALD   What did he do during the war?

ANNA   I'm not sure exactly. When I was growing up, he
            always had a different story. I think it was all
            a cover for his affairs.

            Pause.

DONALD   How long ago were you divorced?

ANNA   Five years ago.

DONALD   Are you with someone now?

ANNA   Not at the moment.... I've become a little burdened
            with the things I want to avoid.

DONALD   Yes I know what you mean.

ANNA   For once, I'd like something to just happen to me.
            Without my anticipating it, or chasing after it, or
            manipulating the situation. Something that just
            crept up on me without my noticing. Like an
            adventure, or a romance.

DONALD   Yes. Like something that happened to people in our
            parent's day.

            Pause.

            Do you like to dance?

ANNA   I love to dance.

DONALD   I haven't been dancing in years.

ANNA   I wouldn't think so. Not at your age.

            DONALD laughs.

DONALD   You seem like such an easygoing person.

ANNA   Are you checking off your list?

DONALD   What list?

ANNA   Your list of qualities that you like in a person.

DONALD   I'm not that calculating.

ANNA   Would you settle for someone who had less than
            half the qualities on your list?

DONALD   At my age, yes.

ANNA   You'll never fall in love that way.

DONALD   Why not?

ANNA   Love isn't a matter of one quality more or less.
            That's why it can last when a couple grows old,
            even when most of the qualities that brought them
            together are gone…. Because it's a union of souls.

DONALD   You must have been talking to Reverend Hill. He's
            always lecturing me about the soul.

            ANNA laughs.

ANNA   I can't explain it… but whenever Reverend Hill
            talks I have an uncontrollable urge to laugh.

DONALD   Why?

ANNA   I don't know.

DONALD   I don't find him all that funny.

ANNA   He reminds me of you.

DONALD   What?

ANNA   You're both very serious.

DONALD   I don't think I'm anything like him.

ANNA   I suppose not. He's always on the verge of crying.
I don't think he's suited for his job.

DONALD   I'm very emotional too.

ANNA   Yes... you are. You're very protective of your
mother.... You must love her very deeply.

    Pause.

    How long ago did your father die?

DONALD   Six months.

ANNA   Were you close?

DONALD   My father was the moral centre of my life. He
endured things that would have broken my spirit.
The world doesn't have heroes like my father
anymore... I miss him.

ANNA   The other day you were telling me a story. About
something that happened to your father during the
war.

DONALD   Oh yes.

My father was only 19 years old when he was sent
to Hong Kong. His company was assigned to
defend a bridge on the outskirts of the city.
Sometimes I try to imagine how he must have felt.
Ten thousand miles from his home. Huddled in the
dark with the other men… boys really… they could
hear the Japanese soldiers creeping along the far
side of the river. The Company Commander
ordered my father to set up a mortar and fire it in
the dark. The first shell hit a branch and…

> *TAMMY enters carrying a garbage pail. She shows
> ANNA the contents of the pail.*

TAMMY   Your father's been smoking in his room.

ANNA   Where did he get the cigarettes?

TAMMY   He says you bought them for him.

ANNA   He must be leaving the home somehow. I'll come
and speak to him. (*to DONALD*) I'm sorry.

DONALD   That's alright. I should wake my mother up. Before
it's time for her to go to bed.

Scene 8

CLARA and PATRICK are making crafts with modelling clay and popsicle sticks. AGNES sits at a separate table, in front of a jigsaw puzzle.

TAMMY   You should start by finding all the pieces with a straight edge.

AGNES   Why should I do that?

TAMMY   Those are the ones that go around the outside.

TAMMY picks up several pieces.

They make the border of the picture. See?

Pause. AGNES stares at the pieces TAMMY has put together.

AGNES   I'd like to go to my room now.

TAMMY   Then you'll say you want to come back.

AGNES   I'm sick and tired of these games. I'm a senior citizen and I'd like to be treated like one.

TAMMY moves to CLARA's table.

TAMMY   (*to CLARA*) How's my angel this morning?

CLARA   Very well, thank you.

TAMMY   Has Patrick been behaving himself?

CLARA   No.

TAMMY   I'm very disappointed in you, Patrick.

CLARA   I told him he would have to be patient. With
           someone like me there's less to tell. So it takes me
           longer to open up.

TAMMY   (*to PATRICK*) Patrick, if anyone finds out you've
           been going out to buy cigarettes, they'll lock you
           upstairs.

PATRICK   I'll stop smoking. (*to CLARA*) For you.

           REVEREND HILL enters.

REVEREND   Good morning everyone!

CLARA   Hello, Reverend Hill.

REVEREND   I can see everyone is hard at work today. Tammy
           keeps you very busy.

CLARA   Yes, she does.

REVEREND   What's that you're making, Patrick?

PATRICK   A tesseract.

REVEREND   Pardon me?

PATRICK   A four dimensional cube.

REVEREND   I was never much good at mathematics. Although
           it's all part of God's intricate design. I'm glad to see
           you're working in clay again, Clara.

CLARA   It's like when you were little. And you could put
           your hands in the mud.

REVEREND   (*to PATRICK*) Has Clara shown you any of her
           creations?

PATRICK   Not yet.

REVEREND   I've offered to be her agent. And I explained to her that an agent gets 90%.

> *REVEREND HILL laughs at his joke.*

TAMMY   (*to AGNES*) Why don't you try putting these two pieces together?

AGNES   Why don't you go to hell?

REVEREND   It's so important to have a hobby as you grow older. One of my parishioners became seriously depressed after he retired. He tried everything—therapy, medication… nothing seemed to help. One day he developed an interest in history and it's made all the difference. He's deeply engaged in his research on the Holocaust now and I think that's made him a lot happier.

CLARA   That's wonderful.

REVEREND   Don't let me keep you from your work.

AGNES   Where's Mrs. O'Neill? Why isn't she here?

TAMMY   She died last night.

CLARA   Oh. That's terrible.

AGNES   How did she die?

REVEREND   She died very peacefully and quietly in her sleep.

AGNES   At least she doesn't have to do crafts anymore.

REVEREND   There will be a memorial service for her in the common room on Friday. Her friends and family will share some stories and memories if you'd like to participate.

CLARA   I didn't know her very well but she was very
          pleasant.

REVEREND (*with tears in his eyes*) Yes. She was an extremely
          pleasant woman…. How are you getting along with
          your puzzle, Agnes?

AGNES   Terrible.

REVEREND It looks like you've made a very good start.

AGNES   I've been here all morning. Too long.

REVEREND You've assembled quite a few pieces.

AGNES   I need you to get me out of here.

REVEREND Is it a mountain scene?

AGNES   I have no idea what it is.

REVEREND Have you looked at the picture on the lid?

AGNES   There is no lid.

TAMMY   It's right in front of you, Agnes.

          *TAMMY turns over the lid and shows it to
          AGNES.*

AGNES   I was much better at this when I was a child.

REVEREND I expect you were a very clever child.

AGNES   I was one of those children who would disappear
          and find a hill somewhere just outside of town. I'd
          spend the day writing stories in my head…. My
          father would call me. When it was time to come
          home.

AGNES looks at her feet.

My socks keep falling down. I told them I like the ones with elastics. They can't seem to remember anything here. I'm sick and tired of these games.

AGNES knocks the puzzle box off the table.

TAMMY   I'll take you to your room, Agnes.

AGNES   I'd like to finish my puzzle.

                TAMMY picks up the pieces of the puzzle.
                DONALD enters.

DONALD   Hello, Mom.

CLARA   Hello, dear? Is it time for bed?

DONALD   Not yet. It's 11:30 in the morning.

CLARA   Why are you here so early?

DONALD   I didn't have to teach today. So I thought I'd surprise you. I'm taking you out for lunch.

REVEREND   Isn't that wonderful, Clara.

DONALD   I've already made a reservation for two at your favourite restaurant.

CLARA   For two?

DONALD   Yes.

CLARA   Isn't Patrick coming?

DONALD   Not today, Mom.

CLARA   Do you have other plans, Patrick?

PATRICK No.

CLARA Then why don't you come?

PATRICK I wasn't invited.

Pause.

DONALD (*to TAMMY*) Is my mother ready to go?

TAMMY Yes. (*to CLARA*) I'll get your coat, Clara.

TAMMY exits.

REVEREND Isn't this a wonderful surprise, Clara? Your son is taking you out to lunch. (*to DONALD*) I thought I should let you know, this Sunday I'll be paying tribute to your father.

DONALD Thank you.

REVEREND I've often wondered how I would stand up in the face of the things he endured. As Pericles said "The man who can most truly be accounted brave, is he who knows best the meaning of what is sweet in life and of what is terrible, and then goes out determined to meet what is to come." Of course you see exactly the same kind of heroism right here in this room. If I was suddenly crippled and had to live in constant pain, I'd think I'd suffered the fate of Job. But old people endure worse things with hardly a complaint.

CLARA Will you be coming to the ceremony, Patrick?

PATRICK No.

CLARA Why not?

PATRICK There's nothing I care to remember.

REVEREND   Were you a combatant during the war?

PATRICK   No.

REVEREND   But you're a veteran…. You must have had some
experiences that you'd like to share with our
congregation.

CLARA   That's right, Patrick.

REVEREND   The outcome of the war wasn't entirely decided on
the field of battle. On Remembrance Day, I also
honour the men and women who played their part
behind the scenes. You may not have risked your
life as a soldier, but every clerk and factory worker
was a hero in their way. You should be proud of
your role in the war, no matter how insignificant it
might seem to you.

PATRICK   My role wasn't insignificant.

REVEREND   I'm sorry. I didn't mean to imply that it was.

PATRICK   I broke an important code.

REVEREND   Really?

　　　　　　TAMMY enters with CLARA's coat.

I think our congregation would be very keen to
hear about the part you played in the war. Thanks
to mathematicians like you, the Allies knew what
the Germans were planning throughout the second
half of the war. You may well have saved thousands
of lives.

PATRICK   (*looking at CLARA*) Yes. But I lost my own.

REVEREND   What do you mean by that?

PATRICK takes CLARA's hand.

DONALD   We should go, Mom.

CLARA   I'd like Patrick to come.

DONALD   He'll be here when you get back.

CLARA   Will you wait for me, Patrick?

PATRICK   Yes. I'll be waiting.

CLARA   Do you promise?

PATRICK   Yes.

AGNES   She's only going for lunch.

PATRICK   Good-bye, my darling.

Scene 9

TAMMY is getting CLARA ready for bed. She holds up a blue dressing gown.

TAMMY   What do you think? It's your favourite colour.

CLARA   It's beautiful…. Whose is it?

TAMMY   Yours.

CLARA   Is it new?

TAMMY   Yes.

CLARA   I don't remember buying it.

TAMMY   I picked it up this afternoon…. It was on sale.

CLARA   Why did you do that?

TAMMY   So you can look your best.

CLARA   Is my son coming?

TAMMY   No, not this evening.

TAMMY helps CLARA into her dressing gown. REVEREND HILL enters.

REVEREND   Knock, knock. I hope everyone is decent.

CLARA   Hello, Reverand Hill.

REVEREND   Hello, Clara.

TAMMY   (*looking at her watch*) I'm just putting Clara to bed.

REVEREND   I won't stay long. I'd like to sit down if you don't mind. You look beautiful Clara. How was your bath?

CLARA   I've been scrubbed from top to bottom.

REVEREND   Is that a new dressing gown?

CLARA   Yes. So I can look my best.

REVEREND   Is your son coming this evening?

CLARA   No.

REVEREND   He visits you almost every day.

CLARA   I don't know what I did to deserve so much attention.

REVEREND   You don't have to do anything to earn the love of your child. You can be a miserable failure in the estimation of the public, but in the eyes of your child you're still the most important person in the world.... Not that you're a miserable failure, Clara.

TAMMY   Have you been drinking?

REVEREND   I've just come from Mrs. O'Neill's wake.

TAMMY starts straightening CLARA's bed.

My goodness, Clara, your bed is a mess. Have you been having an affair?

CLARA   I don't believe in sex before marriage.

TAMMY   Then you'll have to get married.

CLARA   Aren't I too old to be married?

TAMMY   Reverend Hill has married dozens of couples older
               than you.

REVEREND   I'm not sure that Clara is ready for marriage quite
               yet. She would have have to ask permission from
               her son. He has power of attorney.

TAMMY   It's past Clara's bedtime.

REVEREND   Yes I should go. Into the dark, cold night.

               TAMMY continues to straighten CLARA's bed.

               Watching you make Clara's bed has given me an
               idea for a sermon.

TAMMY   Don't you ever relax?

REVEREND   No. I'm afraid I'm condemned to find a moral in
               everything.

               Pause.

               There's only one way to make a bed. The pillow
               goes at the head. The sheets go under the blankets.
               And then, inevitably, the blankets and sheets are
               pulled up to meet the pillow. I'm not sure why, but
               apparently there's no comparison between order
               and disorder... there are just so many more ways...
               I think almost an infinite number of ways... for the
               world to be a complete and utter mess.

TAMMY   No wonder you're losing your congregation.

               PATRICK enters.

REVEREND   Hello, Patrick. What are you doing here? Are you
               lost?

PATRICK   It's nine o'clock.

REVEREND   Yes. And you're in Clara's room.

PATRICK   We have an appointment.

REVEREND   An appointment? But it's time for you and Clara to go to bed.

PATRICK   That's why I'm here.

REVEREND   Come along, Patrick. I'll take you back to your room.

PATRICK   I'd like to stay.

TAMMY   Why don't we leave them alone?

REVEREND   Do you think that's a good idea?

TAMMY   They're adults.

REVEREND   But the rules of the home are quite strict.

TAMMY   Let them have a little time together.

REVEREND   Alright. But I think we should stay too.

Everyone sits uncomfortably.

Why don't you tell us about the code you broke Patrick? You must have known Alan Turing?

PATRICK   Yes.

REVEREND   I expect he would have overseen your work. What was he like?

PATRICK   Why do you want to know?

REVEREND   One of my hobbies is collecting stories about the war.

PATRICK I'm not a hero.

TAMMY I have surprise for you, Clara.

> *TAMMY takes a tape of old dance music from the forties and a small tape deck from her bag. She shows CLARA the tape.*

I'm afraid it's a little worn. I hope it doesn't break.

> *TAMMY puts the tape in the deck.*

REVEREND When I like a song I'll play it over and over for three weeks. And then I can't hear it in the same way anymore.

> *TAMMY pushes the play button.*

Oh my... that's lovely. Does that bring back memories Clara?

CLARA Yes. Do you remember this song, Patrick?

PATRICK Yes. Of course.

CLARA It was my favourite song.

PATRICK Yes. I know.

TAMMY Why don't you ask her to dance, Patrick?

PATRICK I'm not much of a dancer.

TAMMY (*taking PATRICK's hands*) It's easy. You just have to step like this.... (*TAMMY begins to dance with PATRICK.*) Pretend I'm your date. That's it... you're getting the hang of it. You look very dashing in your officers uniform. (*looking at CLARA*) And suddenly, across a crowded room, you catch her eye... the woman you've been waiting for your entire life.... Here, Clara. I'll help you up.

> *TAMMY helps PATRICK hold CLARA.*

You'll have to hold her tight.

> *PATRICK and CLARA dance, with TAMMY*
> *supporting them. ANNA enters and watches*
> *CLARA and PATRICK dance.*

REVEREND   There was a time, a hundred years ago, when people had to wait a long time to hear their favourite song. Sometimes they would wait several years between one peformance and another. And sometimes they might only hear a song once.

> *Pause.*

Imagine how well you would listen if you thought you were hearing a song for the last time. All the cares and resentments of your daily life would seem so unimportant. You'd let go of any thoughts that might distract you from the song. You would almost forget who you were.

> *AGNES enters.*

AGNES   Would you mind keeping the noise down in here? I'm trying to sleep.

> *TAMMY turns off the music.*

REVEREND   (*seeing ANNA*) Yes, I think it's time for everyone to go to bed.

Scene 10

ANNA and DONALD sit in the common room of the nursing home.

ANNA   Is something the matter? You seem very preoccupied.

DONALD   No. I'm fine.

ANNA   Is your mother sleeping?

DONALD   She wasn't in her room. She must be having a bath.

          ANNA looks at her watch.

          Where's your father?

ANNA   He wasn't in his room either…. (*laughing*) Maybe we should try to find our parents.

DONALD   Yes.

          Pause.

ANNA   My father seems to have taken quite a liking to your mother.

DONALD   Yes.

ANNA   I hope that doesn't bother you. I know your father passed away recently.

DONALD   I'm sure it's not very serious. My mother isn't really herself. Sometimes she thinks my father is still alive and that they're still living in their old house. You might warn your father to be little cautious. He may be hurt if he gets too attached.

ANNA   My father seems to think he knew your mother during the war.

DONALD   Where was he stationed?

ANNA   Near Toronto. Before he was sent overseas.

DONALD   I don't know how they would have met. My mother lived on a farm near Windsor. She and my father were married a week before he was shipped to Hong Kong. During his imprisonment he lost over forty pounds. He contracted rickets and malaria. And he was beaten mercilessly by the guards. But he wrote in his diary "We are determined to bear our humiliation without a murmur." My mother didn't receive a letter from him for two years. She didn't know if he was alive or dead. But she never lost hope.

ANNA   They must have been deeply in love.

DONALD   Yes. They were. Their marriage was the most consistent thing in my life.

         TAMMY enters. She walks past DONALD and ANNA and is about to exit.

         Hello, Tammy. Have you seen my mother?

TAMMY   She's in the basement.

DONALD   What's she doing in the basement?

TAMMY   Dancing.

DONALD   With who?

TAMMY   Patrick.

         TAMMY exits.

ANNA   Well, at least they're having fun.

DONALD   I think Tammy is stealing money from my mother.

ANNA   What makes you think she's stealing money?

DONALD   She buys things with my mother's money, but she never keeps the receipts. And everything she buys is twice as expensive as you'd expect.

ANNA   You should tell the Director. There may have been other complaints.

DONALD   But my mother loves her. What if they let her go? It's terrible not knowing what kind of a person she is…. I'm a terrible coward.

ANNA   Why do you say that?

DONALD   I spend half of my visits sitting in this chair. I find it hard to see my mother in the condition she's in.

ANNA   But she seems quite healthy.

DONALD   She can tell you which dress she was wearing the day my father came home from war. But not what she did yesterday.

            Pause.

            Do you remember the saddest day of your life?

ANNA   There've been so many.

DONALD   But if you had to choose.

ANNA   I suppose it was the day my daughter stopped talking out-loud when she played.

DONALD   Your life is hardly the stuff great tragedies are made
          of.

ANNA   Yes, but it was very sad.

DONALD   This happened on a particular day?

ANNA   Yes. And the worst thing is, I think I caused it.

DONALD   How?

ANNA   My daughter and I had just come home from her
          cousin's fourth birthday party. She said her cousin
          was so cute because she always did the voices for
          her dolls and animals when she played. I said "Just
          like you." and she looked stunned. It was the first
          time she was aware that she spoke out-loud when
          she played. After that she always played with her
          toys in complete silence. I couldn't hear what she
          was thinking anymore.

          Pause.

DONALD   This summer, at the cottage, I was aware that I was
          having fun, but my enjoyment was always
          overshadowed by so many concerns—worries
          about the future, about my daughter Nina, my
          work, even worries about the way our activities
          were effecting the lake—there were huge
          boathouses springing up everywhere—all part of
          the relentless development of the north. But looking
          back, a few weeks later, I cried—I felt the pure joy
          of watching Nina jump into the water over and
          over. I remembered the way she and her friends
          named every dive—"The pencil." "The chair."
          "The dead man."—even though every dive was
          essentially the same, but the way they laughed, the
          way they shouted out the names, the anticipation…
          it was so simple… they will never be happier—
          I cried for that, because it was so simple and so

hard to reproduce—because it would never happen again.... People should be put to death at age ten.... What purpose does growing old serve?

ANNA   Maybe the purpose of life isn't ultimately to be happy or to suffer, but to do both at the same time. Children can never experience the incredible bittersweetness of joy and pain at the same time, of life lived in retrospect, the awareness of things passing—for that you need memory—you need to grow old.

    Pause.

My father would like to marry your mother.

DONALD   You're not serious are you?

ANNA   I think, it's something we should consider.

Scene 11

DONALD paces back and forth in front of a door with a small stained glass window. He opens the door a crack. We hear organ music. DONALD closes the door. AGNES approaches.

AGNES   Am I late?

DONALD   The service just started.

AGNES   Aren't you going in?

DONALD   No. Not at the moment.

Pause. AGNES looks at the door.

AGNES   Is it safe?

DONALD   Safe? Oh… yes. I'm just stretching my legs.

AGNES continues to look at the door.

There's nothing wrong. It's just a service. Just a bunch of people sitting in pews.

AGNES opens the door to the church. We hear the REVEREND's voice.

REVEREND   Rats as big as dogs, gorging themselves on human flesh in no man's land…

AGNES enters the church. DONALD continues to pace. A few moments later AGNES opens the door to the church.

6 million Jews, 20 million Russians, 50 million Chinese…

> AGNES *glares at* DONALD *and leaves the church.*
> ANNA *and* PATRICK *enter.* PATRICK *is wearing*
> *his uniform.*

DONALD   Hello, Patrick. You look very dashing. My God,
            look at all those medals. What's this one for?

PATRICK   Keeping my mouth shut.

ANNA   Why don't you go in, Dad? I'll join you in a minute.

> PATRICK *opens the door and enters the church.*

REVEREND   ...every day is like an endless trip to the
            laundromat, we can never get all of our chores
            done...

ANNA   Where's your mother?

DONALD   Inside.

ANNA   Why aren't you with her?

DONALD   I find it hard to listen to Reverend Hill's sermons.
            I guess it reminds me of my childhood.

> *Pause.*

ANNA   My father was very hurt by your decision. He
            doesn't understand how you could object to their
            marriage.... Haven't you seen them together?
            They're like little children.

DONALD   Yes. They are. And I find it extremely sad.

ANNA   But your mother is so happy.

DONALD   That's because her mind is barely functioning.

ANNA   Functioning?

DONALD   Yes.

ANNA   You talk about her like she's a machine. What percent of her would you say is still operating?

           Pause.

DONALD   Even if my mother was more herself, I'm afraid I couldn't allow her to marry your father.

ANNA   Why not?

DONALD   Your father is hardly a suitable match.

ANNA   Why do you say that?

DONALD   He's an alcoholic and a womaniser.

ANNA   A womaniser?

DONALD   Yes.

ANNA   He's 82.

           Pause.

           He's taking his medication regularly for the first time in his life. He hasn't tried to escape or go drinking since he came here. He's even started to talk to me. He's told me stories about his childhood and the war that have made me see him differently.

DONALD   Why is he so determined to marry my mother?

ANNA   He wants to walk down the aisle with his bride. To wake up every morning beside her. To cherish and care for her. Until the day he dies. You may not understand it, but it means something to them. It's his last chance to share a life with someone.

DONALD   I'm sorry, but my mother is far too vulnerable.

> *ANNA turns and opens the door to the church. We hear an elderly congregation singing. ANNA enters the church.*

CONGREGATION
>A thousand ages in thy sight
>Are like an evening gone;
>Short as the watch that ends the night
>Before the rising sun.

> *The music fades slowly as the door closes. Moments later ANNA comes rushing out through the door.*

ANNA   My father is gone.

Scene 12

PATRICK is tied to a chair with restraining straps.
He is still wearing his uniform. He has a large
bruise on his face. DONALD enters.

DONALD   Hello, Patrick. Where did they find you? (*noticing*
          PATRICK's face) Did you have a fall?

PATRICK   (*indicating the straps*) Would you mind cutting
          these?

DONALD   I think I should ask a nurse.

PATRICK   It's alright.

DONALD   Where do you want to go?

PATRICK   I don't want to go anywhere. I just don't like being
          tied up.

          Pause.

DONALD   Listen, Patrick… I'm sorry… about my decision…
          but if I allowed you to marry my mother,
          I wouldn't be living up to my responsibilities
          as a son. She's not fully herself.

PATRICK   We made love.

DONALD   What?

PATRICK   She asked me to. So I put her on the bed and
          straightened her out. She…

DONALD   I don't think I need to know the details.

PATRICK   We're adults…. We know what we want. I'm the
          only person she ever loved.

DONALD   Do you think so?

PATRICK   Yes.

DONALD   I'm afraid that's not true, Patrick. My mother loved
           my father. They were married before he went to
           war.

PATRICK   She thought he was dead.

DONALD   Your daughter says you tend to make up stories.

PATRICK   This one's true.

DONALD   Then why didn't you come back for her after the
           war?

PATRICK   I couldn't.

DONALD   Why not?

PATRICK   My superiors wanted me to stay overseas. They
           needed me.

DONALD   What for?

PATRICK   I served my country. I don't have to tell you the
           details.

DONALD   My mother lived on a farm with her parents, you
           weren't stationed anywhere near her. How could
           you...

           ANNA enters.

ANNA   Hello.

DONALD   Hello.

           Pause.

(*very uncomfortable*) I was just talking to your father. (*indicating PATRICK's straps*) He wants someone to remove his straps.

ANNA   I don't think so.

PATRICK   Why not?

ANNA   They don't want to lose you again.

DONALD   They can't keep him tied up forever.

ANNA   (*to DONALD*) He's being moved to the second floor this afternoon.

DONALD   Why are they doing that?

ANNA   (*looking at her father*) They've decided he's a danger to himself.

DONALD   But surely that's up to you to decide.

ANNA   It's not up to me. If he drinks again it could kill him.

          Pause.

Don't worry. It's not your fault... if that's what you're concerned about. It was an impractical idea. I'm sorry I encouraged it.

Scene 13

*REVEREND HILL and DONALD sit in the
common room of the home.*

REVEREND   I enjoy our conversations. I feel a little out of place
in this town. The deciding issue in the last election
was snowmobile trails.

Pause.

DONALD   How do you know when God is talking to you?

REVEREND   God doesn't talk to me. Not personally. As Paul
said, "we only see him through a glass darkly."

DONALD   But then he only sees us through a glass darkly.

REVEREND   No. I believe he sees us as we truly are.

Pause.

DONALD   Have you seen Patrick?

REVEREND   Yes. I saw him this morning.

DONALD   How is he?

REVEREND   I think he's adjusting.

DONALD   Do you think I'm a terrible person?

REVEREND   Why would I think that?

DONALD   I've made a lot of people unhappy.

REVEREND   I'm sure that wasn't your intention.

DONALD   No. But I don't think Anna will ever forgive me.

REVEREND   Patrick is an adult. He made a decision to go
            drinking. In the end only God can understand or
            forgive a person's motivations.

DONALD   That's a convenient way to ease your conscience.
            What if there is no God?

REVEREND   A Russian novelist—I believe it was Dostoyevski—
            said that if there is no God then everything is
            permitted. But I think it's even worse than that.
            Because if there is no God, then everything will be
            forgotten.

DONALD   Yes. I agree. But that's simply the way the world
            happens to be. There's no point inventing an
            omniscient God to console yourself. Even the most
            powerful computer has to clear it's memory when
            it's full. You can't have consciousness without
            constant loss.

REVEREND   So what do you live for? What will survive of the
            things you devoted yourself to? I couldn't live
            without the faith that there's something more
            permanent than us. Something that watches and
            remembers.

DONALD   To be honest, I don't know what I'm living for.
            I used to think it was my work. But I'm too old to
            do anything remarkable now. And when people do
            finally understand the mind they'll build
            computers or neural implants that will make us all
            look like Neanderthals. Then there's my daughter.
            But she barely has time to see me anymore.

REVEREND   How old is she?

DONALD   Ten. And then there's my mother. But unfortunately
            she's dying. And when she's dead, no one will ever
            think of me the way she did again…. Not even
            God.

Pause. TAMMY enters.

REVEREND   How's Agnes?

TAMMY   Doctor Stevens thinks you should see her.

REVEREND   I'll be right there

TAMMY exits.

If you need someone to talk to, I would be happy to talk. I won't try to convert you.

DONALD   You won't be able to help it. What else do you have to offer besides faith?

REVEREND   Just my friendship.

Scene 14

DONALD watches CLARA sleeping.

DONALD   Hello, Mom.

CLARA   Hello, dear.

DONALD   Sorry I'm late. The traffic was bad.

CLARA   It was nice of you to come.

DONALD   How was your day?

CLARA   Wonderful.

DONALD   Did you do anything special?

CLARA   No.... Not that I can remember.

DONALD   How are you feeling?

CLARA   Fine.

DONALD shows CLARA a postcard.

DONALD   Another postcard from the Copes. There's a picture
            of a cave on the front. They're in Southern
            California now. Would you like me to read it?

CLARA   Yes. Please.

DONALD   "Dear Clara, hope you are well. We visited the
            Carlsbad Caverns today. Look forward to seeing
            you when we return on the 15th. Love Jim and
            Marjorie...." I'm sure they'll have lots of news
            when they get back.

            *DONALD opens CLARA's drawer and puts the
            postcard inside.*

We really have to organise this drawer Mom. Maybe on the weekend.... I have a meeting with the president of the university tomorrow morning. I think he's going to ask me to be the head of the psychology department.

CLARA   That's good. You can change all those crazy things the first years have to do.

DONALD   What crazy things?

CLARA   All those pranks.

DONALD   They're not going to put me in charge of orientation Mom. I'll be the youngest chair at the university. It's something I'm really proud of.

CLARA   On the first day of school you were so frightened. All the other children were running and screaming. You wouldn't let go of my leg. The teacher couldn't pull you away.

DONALD   I don't remember that.

CLARA   I had to take you home again.

Pause.

DONALD   How are you feeling?

CLARA   A little sleepy.

DONALD   But you're alright?

CLARA   Yes. Of course. Why shouldn't I be? Why do you keep asking me how I am?

Pause.

DONALD   You didn't drink your juice, Mom.

CLARA   I don't want it.

DONALD   The nurse said, you should drink more.

CLARA   I'll have it at home.

DONALD   This is your home.

CLARA   I mean at my house.

DONALD   We sold your house.

CLARA   Why?

DONALD   You needed help taking care of yourself.

CLARA   I've always taken care of myself.

DONALD   Your memory's not very good anymore, Mom.

CLARA   I can still remember my phone number.

DONALD   What is it?

CLARA   705-635-2063.

DONALD   That's very good, Mom.

           Pause.

           How was dinner?

CLARA   I didn't go.

DONALD   Why not?

CLARA   My date didn't show up.

           Pause.

DONALD   (*shaken*) Why don't you have some juice?

> *DONALD reaches for the juice and knocks it over.*

I'm sorry, Mom. I've made a terrible mess.... I'll get something to clean it up with.

> *DONALD exits. He returns a moment later with a mop and pail.*

(*mopping the floor*) There. At least you won't slip on it.

CLARA   You always take such good care of me.

DONALD   I try my best.

> *Pause.*

You must be starving. I'll go and see if I can get you something to eat. I'll be back soon.

CLARA   Alright.

> *DONALD hugs CLARA. He holds her for several seconds.*

Goodbye, dear.

> *DONALD exits. CLARA sits starting ahead. DONALD reenters.*

DONALD   I forgot my coat.

> *DONALD picks up his coat.*

See you soon.

> *He exits.*

A nurse, DIANA, enters.

DIANA   Hello, dear. I've come to get you ready for bed....
My goodness—your bed's a mess. Have you been
having an affair?

CLARA   Yes.

DIANA   Good for you.

DIANA continues tidying the bed.

CLARA   I don't remember you.

DIANA   I don't usually work on this floor. I'm usually
upstairs.

CLARA   I'd like to go there.

DIANA   Oh, I don't think so, dear.

CLARA   Why not?

DIANA   It's very sad up there. There's one old gentleman
who stands by the door all day asking if he can go
out.

CLARA   Do you think he'll get out?

DIANA   No. He's a drinker. No one will let him out....

Pause. DIANA helps CLARA into bed.

Tammy asked me to say hello.

CLARA   Tammy?

DIANA   She said you were like a second mother to her.

CLARA   Where is she?

DIANA   She has another job.

CLARA   What's she doing?

DIANA   I'm not sure. I think she's in sales.

           Pause. DIANA picks up a picture on CLARA's dresser.

           Is this your son?

CLARA   Yes.

DIANA   He's very handsome.

CLARA   He's gone.

           Pause. CLARA stares at the mop.

           He was the dearest sweetest thing.

DIANA   Oh... I'm sorry

           DIANA notices that CLARA is staring at the mop.

           Someone forgot to put away the mop. I'll get this out of your way, dear.

CLARA   (*indicating the logo on the bucket*) What does this mean?

DIANA   Rubbermaid? It's just the name of the company that made the mop and pail.

CLARA   Oh.

           Pause.

DIANA   I have to get your medicine, dear.

*DIANA exits. CLARA closes her eyes and falls
asleep. PATRICK enters and sits by her bed.
CLARA opens her eyes.*

CLARA   I fell asleep. I just shut my eyes and fell asleep.

PATRICK   So you're feeling better?

CLARA   Oh yes. Sleep is the greatest protection.

Pause.

And when I think about what the pioneers had to
do.

Pause.

It wasn't like it is now…. But the water was clear.

Pause.

I missed you, Patrick.

PATRICK   I missed you too.

Pause.

CLARA   Today was a special day. We had a visit from
a children's choir.

PATRICK   I'm sorry I missed it.

CLARA   The children said we could sing along. For the last
song.

Pause.

I hope they didn't get tired from standing so long.

PATRICK   There's always a danger in that.

CLARA   Isn't it funny, children can never walk. They have to run.

            Pause.

            You don't really remember me do you, Patrick?

PATRICK   Yes. I do.

CLARA   But I didn't mean anything to you.

PATRICK   You meant everything.

            Pause.

CLARA   Do you remember when we first met?

PATRICK   Yes. I was on leave.

CLARA   But you were wearing your officers' uniform.

PATRICK   You were in a blue dress.

CLARA   You were another person's date.

PATRICK   I didn't care about my date. You were so beautiful.

            Pause.

CLARA   A week later you were gone.

PATRICK   I'm sorry. I had to.

CLARA   And I never heard from you again.

            Pause.

            You'll find people never do what you think they should do.

PATRICK   I'm sorry. For everything.

CLARA   I forgive you…. Now we can start over.

              DIANA enters and stares at PATRICK.

DIANA   Hello, Patrick. What are you doing here? You're on
              the wrong floor.

              Pause.

              How did you get down here?

PATRICK   I broke the code.

DIANA   You're very naughty. Now we'll have to change it.

              She takes PATRICK's arm.

              Come along now, dear. We'll find a nurse to take
              you upstairs.

PATRICK   I'd like to stay.

DIANA   It's time for Clara to go to sleep.

PATRICK   She asked me to stay.

DIANA   Oh I couldn't leave you two alone without
              a chaperone.

              Pause.

              Come along, Patrick. It's time to go. I'm on a busy
              shift.

              *DIANA leads PATRICK away. CLARA closes her
              eyes. DIANA enters.*

I'm sorry, Clara. I don't know how he got down here. He seemed very disoriented.

DIANA gives CLARA her medicine.

CLARA   I didn't mind. We're married.

DIANA   Oh, are you? Is he a good husband?

CLARA   Yes.

DIANA   You're lucky then. I wish I could say the same.... Mine has his moments.

DIANA pulls CLARA's blankets up.

Do you like your covers up under your chin?

CLARA   Yes.

DIANA   Just like a little girl.... There, you're all tucked in. I hope you have a beautiful sleep.

CLARA   Thank you.

DIANA   Would you like me to draw the curtain?

CLARA   Yes.

DIANA draws the curtain. We hear CLARA's voice from behind the curtain.

CLARA   What did you say your name was?

DIANA   Diana.

CLARA   I'll try to remember that.

Pause.

Will I see you again tomorrow?

DIANA   I'll be on Patrick's floor tomorrow.

               DIANA exits.

CLARA   I knew a Patrick once during the war.... You would
               be too young to remember.

               Pause.

               Apparently he has a daughter now.

               Pause.

               Of course Dad was on the railroad.... We had a lot
               of miles to walk down the track. But he was good
               company.

               Pause.

               I enjoyed the morning. There were quite a few
               there. Not as many as last year. But there were
               some good singers.

               The lights fade.

For the past seven years, John Mighton has coordinated JUMP, a successful school program designed to tutor children who are having difficulties in math. John has written an inspirational book based on his experiences with JUMP called *The Myth of Ability: Nurturing Mathematical Talent in Every Child*, published by House of Anansi Press.

Mighton completed a Ph.D. in Mathematics at the University of Toronto and has lectured in Philosophy at McMaster University. He held an NSERC postdoctoral fellowship for research in graph theory and knot theory at The Fields Insitute and is currently an Adjunct Professor at the University of Toronto.

Mighton's plays, *Scientific Americans, Possible Worlds, A Short History of Night, Body and Soul* and *The Little Years*, have been performed across Canada, as well as in Europe, Japan and the United States, and have won several national awards including a Governor General's Literary Award for Drama for *Possible Worlds* and *A Short History of Night*.

Mighton's play *Possible Worlds* was made into full-length feature film directed by renowned director/playwright Robert Lepage.